Come With Me

Maggie Walker

It might be best if you stay close by me as we travel through this story. Where does it begin?

It begins, of course, once upon a time – once upon a time in a dark, dark forest.

Once upon a time there was a dark, dark forest.

Can you hear the trees rustle and rattle in the wind?

Look how dark it is. The trees are so thick, the sunlight cannot get through.

Walk with me softly through the dark, dark forest.

In the middle of the dark, dark forest there was a dark, dark house.

Look, it is only a small cottage.

I don't think anyone lives here. The paint has peeled from the doors and there is thick dirt on the windows.

There is a lamp hanging by the door. Let's light it and look inside.

Come on.

Inside the dark, dark house was a dark, dark staircase.

It smells musty and old in here.

There are so many cobwebs, there must be hundreds of spiders.

What was that?

Only a mouse.

Let's go up the stairs, shall we?

Follow me.

At the top of the dark, dark staircase was a dark, dark room.

Look, the door is open. Let's go inside.

I'll hold the lamp up high, it's so dark in here.

There is a bed and an old faded rug.

What is that in the corner?

Let's go and see.

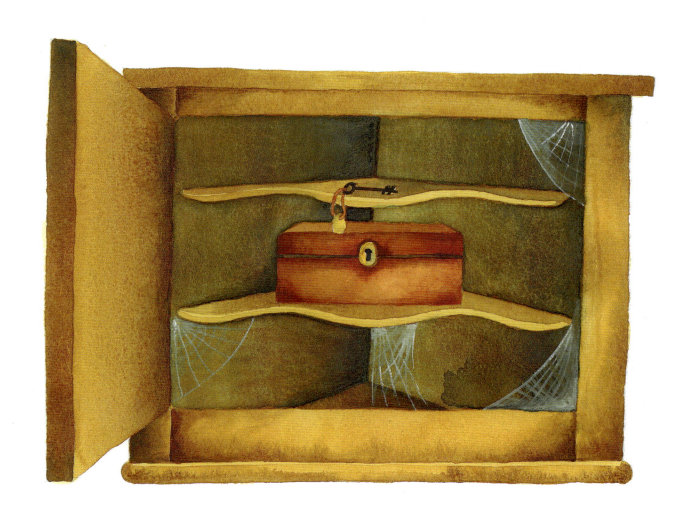

In the dark, dark room there was a dark, dark cupboard.

This cupboard looks as though it's been here for hundreds of years.

It's got strange patterns carved in the wood.

I'll turn the handle and see if it will open.

Creeeeeeeeeeeakkkk.

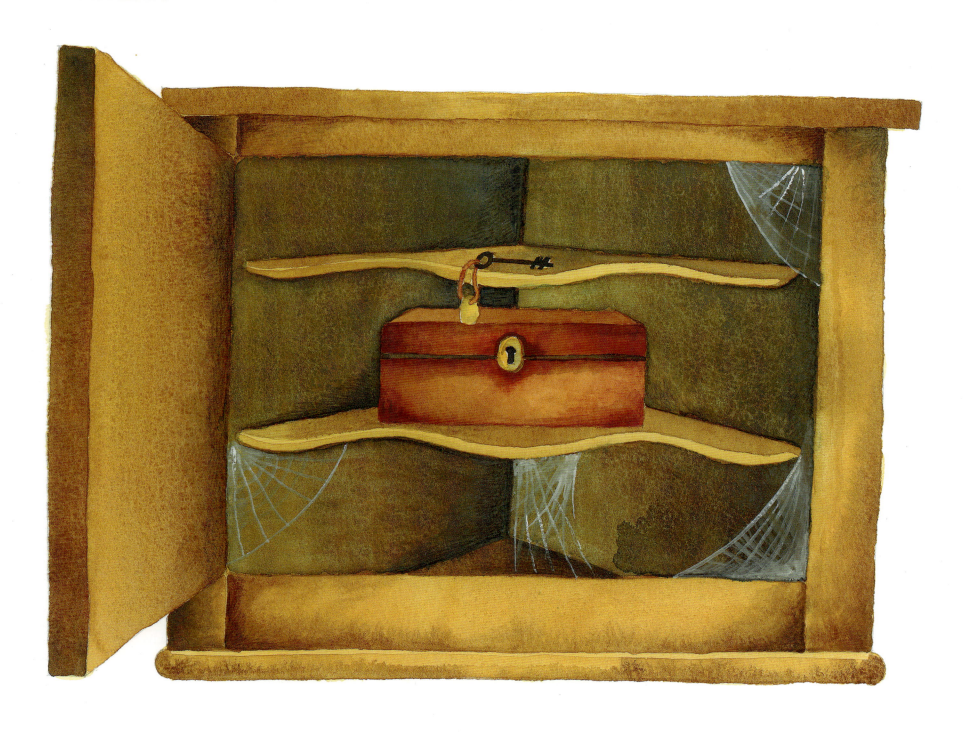

In the dark, dark cupboard there was a dark, dark box.

It's covered in cobwebs, I'll wipe them off.

I can't open it.

Wait, there's a key here on the shelf.

It's a bit rusted. I wonder if it will fit.

Come a bit nearer or you won't see. Yes it fits.

Are you ready for me to open the box?

In the dark, dark box there was a . . .

Aaaaaaaaaaaaaagghhh!!!

Come back! Come back!

Whatever it was, it's gone.

Don't run away now.

Come back and see what is left in the box.

The dark, dark box is full of wishes.

Come back and make a wish.

I wish I had never seen that dark, dark box,

or that dark, dark cupboard,

or that dark, dark room,

or that dark, dark staircase,

or that dark, dark house,

or that dark, dark forest.

I wish I was back home, that's what I wish.

What a waste of a wish.
What will you wish for?